This book is dedicated to a lifetime of love and romance.

Therefore shall a man leave his father and his mother, and shall cleave unto his wife: and they shall be one flesh.

Genesis 2:24 KJV

ii

Index:

At the touch of love everyone becomes a poet. Plato

CHAPTER ONE

The Wedding of the Century

No, not the marriage of William and Kate.   Not the Celebrity of the Month's, either.   Yours!

No matter how simple or elaborate, your ceremony is The Wedding of The Century.

For the past four years I've been a licensed and ordained minister, traveling throughout central and southern Ohio marrying people.   I've been to mansions, conservatories, covered bridges, baseball diamonds, football stadiums, gazebos, back yards, private clubs, churches, back yards, front rooms – even prisons.   Let me share with you things I've learned so that you may have a stress free, meaningful and beautiful ceremony, for The Wedding of the Century.

I love thee, I love but thee
With a love that shall not die
Till the sun grows cold
And the stars grow old.

William Shakespeare

CHAPTER TWO

Lawfully Wedded

Let's get the official, legal basics out of the way before getting to the fun stuff.

As you know, marriage laws vary from state to state. For details, run an Internet search ... "marriage laws" or call Probate Court in the county where you plan to marry.

In order to get married, you need a marriage license. Before applying for your license find out what type of IDs are acceptable along with any residency requirements.

Make sure you get your license in plenty of time, especially if you live in a state that requires a waiting period. However, don't get it too early as licenses expire in many states. (For example, 60 days in Ohio.)

Apply for your license together, and bring identification, previous divorce decrees if applicable, and cash to pay the license fee.

If you have any doubts about the authenticity of your minister's credentials, check them out. If you plan to marry within the state of Ohio query "minister license" at http://www.sos.state.oh.us. If you are not sure how to go about this procedure, a good place to start is the Secretary of State's office.

The wedding officiant is responsible for signing your certificate of marriage and returning it to the court.

CHAPTER THREE

Finding a Minister

If you are not affiliated with a church, or God forbid, your minister declines to marry you for any reason, there are ways to locate an officiant.

The phone book is the first thing that comes to mind, but as that is an expensive way to advertise not all officiants will be listed. Since independent ministers than those affiliated with churches are more likely to meet your needs, you might want to expand your search.

Wedding officiants frequently advertise in local free papers as well as the Internet. Searches of bridal sites will often garner ministers with heftier fees, so if you have a tighter budget, search "minister," "wedding" and "officiant" along with your city and state.

There is always the ever popular word of mouth method of advertising, so ask around.

In some areas, judges will perform marriage ceremonies and in many they will not. Check with the probate court. In one county of Ohio, judges do courthouse weddings but they are booked up for several months and therefore unavailable for last minute weddings. Judges in an adjoining county will not perform courthouse weddings under any circumstances, but do keep a list of licensed ministers who are willing and often eager to perform your ceremony.

Recently a woman called to find out my fee. The only other person she was able to find to drive to her location - all of thirty miles - wanted $425. I laughed. Yes, she booked me.

If you need to meet with the minister before your wedding, be willing to pay a shopper's fee. Although we are very happy for you, our time is valuable as is yours. We have families and full calendars, too. One couple suggested we meet on Easter Sunday afternoon as that was their only time available. They also wanted me to bring pictures of weddings so that I could sell my services.

If you want the officiant to attend a rehearsal, be prepared to pay for his or her time. Rehearsal fees are often an additional one-half of the wedding honorarium. It is thoughtful to invite your officiant to the rehearsal dinner.

If your minister is a seasoned officiant, he or she will not need to attend a rehearsal except under extraordinary circumstances. (I can't think of any, but there is always that possibility.) You and your wedding party may practice as often as you want.

If your minister is writing your vows, ask to have them emailed to you as early as possible. If you are writing your own ceremony, please provide them to the minister so that everything is ready to go.

Feel free to email or call your officiant with any questions. If your minister is judgmental or does not approve of your ceremony or your relationship, consider finding someone else. Remember, you are the star of The Wedding of The Century! (Just don't be a prima donna.)

He felt now that he was not simply close to her, but that he did not know where he ended and she began.

Leo Tolstoy

CHAPTER FOUR

Blessings and Prayers

Apache Wedding Blessing

Now you will feel no rain, for each of you will be shelter for the other. Now you will feel no cold, for each of you will be warmth to the other. Now there will be no loneliness, for each of you will be companion to the other. Now you are two persons, but there is only one life before you. May beauty surround you both in the journey ahead and through all the years. May happiness be your companion and your days together be good and long upon the earth.

Treat yourselves and each other with respect, and remind yourselves often of what brought you together. Give the highest priority to the tenderness, gentleness and kindness that your connection deserves.

When frustration, difficulties and fear assail your relationship, as they threaten all relationships at one time or another, remember to focus on what is right between you, not only the part which seems wrong.

In this way, you can ride out the storms when clouds hide the face of the sun in your lives -- remembering that even if you lose sight of it for a moment, the sun is still there. And if each of you takes responsibility for the quality of your life together, it will be marked by abundance and delight.

Cherokee Wedding Blessing

God in heaven above please protect the ones we love. We honor all you created as we pledge our hearts and lives together. We honor Mother Earth and ask for our marriage to be abundant and grow stronger through the seasons. We honor fire and ask that our union be warm and glowing with love in our hearts. We honor wind and ask that we sail through life safe and calm as in our father's arms. We honor water to clean and soothe our relationship -- that it may never thirst for love. With all the forces of the universe you created, we pray for harmony as we grow forever young together.   Amen.

The Way (Anonymous)

The way is long -- let us go together
The way is difficult -- let us help each other
The way is joyful -- let us share it
The way is ours alone -- let us go in love
The way grows before us -- let us begin

Native American Prayer

O Great Spirit, whose breath gives life to the world, and whose voice is heard in the soft breeze:

We need your strength and wisdom.

Cause us to walk in beauty.

Give us eyes ever to behold the red and purple sunset.

Make us wise so that we may understand what you have taught us.

Help us learn the lessons you have hidden in every leaf and rock.

Make us always ready to come to you with clean hands and steady eyes, so when life fades, like the fading sunset, our spirits may come to you without shame.

Blessing (Anonymous)

May your home be filled with laughter and the warm embrace of a summer day.

May you find peacefulness and beauty, challenge, and satisfaction, humor and insight, healing and renewal, love and wisdom, as in a quiet heart.

May you always feel that what you have is enough.

The Lord's Prayer

Our Father who art in heaven,

Hallowed be thy name,

Thy kingdom come,

Thy will be done in earth, as it is in heaven.

Give us this day our daily bread.

And forgive us our debts,

as we forgive our debtors.

And lead us not into temptation,

but deliver us from evil:

For thine is the kingdom,

and the power, and the glory forever

Amen

Irish Wedding Blessing

May God be with you and bless you;

May you see your children's children.

May you be poor in misfortune,

Rich in blessings,

May you know nothing but happiness

From this day forward.

May the sun shine warm upon your face,

The rains fall soft upon your fields.

And until we meet again,

May God hold you in the palm of his hand.

Navajo Wedding Blessing

Now you have lit a fire and that fire should not go out.

The two of you now have a fire that represents love,
understanding and a philosophy of life.

It will give you heat, food, warmth and happiness.

The new fire represents a new beginning - a new life and a new family.

The fire should keep burning; you should stay together.

You have lit the fire for life, until old age separates you.

Jewish Wedding Blessing

He who is the Al-mighty

and Omnipotent, over all;

He who is Blessed, over all;

He who is the Greatest of all;

He who is Distinguished of all;

Shall Bless the Chosson and Kallah.

An Irish Wedding Prayer

By the power that Christ brought from heaven,

mayst thou love me.

As the sun follows its course,

mayst thou follow me.

As light to the eye,

as bread to the hungry,

as joy to the heart,

may thy presence be with me,

oh one that I love,

'til death comes to part us asunder.

Scottish Wedding Blessing

May joy and peace surround you both,

Contentment latch your door,

May happiness be with you now;

God bless you evermore.

A Polish Blessing

Lord, we ask you to bless this family

With a warm place by the fire

When the world is cold,

A light in the window when the way is dark,

A welcoming smile when the road is long,

A haven of love when the day is done.

For the blessing of this home we give thanks.

German Wedding Blessing

With faith there is love,

With love there is peace,

With peace there is blessing,

With blessing, there is God,

With God there is no need.

A Wedding Prayer

by Robert Louis Stevenson

Lord, behold our family here assembled.

We thank you for this place in which we dwell,

for the love that unites us,

for the peace accorded us this day,

for the hope with which we expect the morrow,

---

for the health, the work, the food,

and the bright skies that make our lives delightful;

for our friends in all parts of the earth.   Amen.

Catholic Wedding Prayer

Father, when you created mankind you willed that man and wife should be one.

Bind [groom] and [bride] in the loving union of marriage; and make their love fruitful so that they may be living witnesses to your divine love in the world.

We ask this through our Lord Jesus Christ, your Son,

who lives and reigns with you and the Holy Spirit,

one God, for ever and ever.   Amen.

Native American Blessing

Great Spirit, Grant that our hearts may always be young and that our dreams may last forever.

Hindu Marriage Poem

You have become mine forever.

Yes, we have become partners.

I have become yours.

Hereafter, I cannot live without you.

Do not live without me.

Let us share the joys.

We are word and meaning, unite.

You are thought and I am sound.

May the nights be honey-sweet for us.

May the mornings be honey-sweet for us.

May the plants be honey-sweet for .

May the earth be honey-sweet for us.

Muslim Marriage Poem

May your vows and this marriage be blessed.

May it be sweet milk, this marriage, sweet drink and halvah.

May this marriage offer fruit and shade like the date palm.

May this marriage be full of laughter, your every day a day in paradise.

May this marriage be a sign of compassion, a seal of happiness here and hereafter.

May this marriage have a fair face and a good name, an omen as welcome as the moon in a clear evening sky....

May Spirit enter and mingle in this marriage.

A Reading from 1 Corinithian 13:4-13

Love is patient, love is kind. It does not envy, it does not boast, it is not proud. It is not rude, it is not self-seeking, it is not easily angered, it keeps no record of wrongs. Love does not delight in evil but rejoices with the truth. It always protects, always trusts, always hopes, always perseveres. Love never fails.

But where there are prophecies, they will cease; where there are tongues, they will be stilled; where there is knowledge, it will pass away.

—

For we know in part and we prophesy in part, but when perfection comes, the imperfect disappears.

When I was a child, I talked like a child, I thought like a child, I reasoned like a child. When I became a man, I put childish ways behind me. Now we see but a poor reflection as in a mirror; then we shall see face to face. Now I know in part; then I shall know fully, even as I am fully known. And now these three remain: faith, hope and love. But the greatest of these is love.

Prayer of Peace - St. Francis

Lord make me an instrument of your peace
Where there is hatred,
Let me sow love;
Where there is injury, pardon;
Where there is doubt, faith;
Where there is despair, hope;
Where there is darkness, light;
And where there is sadness, Joy.
O Divine Master grant that I may
Not so much seek to be consoled
As to console;
To be understood,
As to understand;
To be loved as to love.
For it is in giving that we receive,
It is in pardoning that we are pardoned.

And it is in dying that we are

Born to eternal life. Amen

Matthew 19:6 - So they are no longer two, but one.
Therefore what God has joined together, let man not
separate.

CHAPTER FIVE

Traditions and Superstitions

Tossing the bouquet dates from the time when a bride considered herself lucky to have caught a man.

According to tradition, the woman who catches the bouquet will be the next to marry.

Stand with your back to your guests and fling your bouquet over your shoulder.

You can have a nosegay created just for this purpose and either keep your bridal bouquet or present it to your grandmother, mother, aunt or other loved one.

The garter toss is a fun way to get single men involved in the reception. Wear two garters, one to fling and one to keep, on your right leg. Your groom will turn his back on the men and toss the garter over his head toward them.

The garter and bridal bouquet winner can be photographed together. They also can have a special dance after the father/daughter dance, and the garter guy can put the garter on the bouquet gal.

Superstitions are for entertainment only, so don't take them seriously.

Whether tying tin cans to the back of the "getaway car" to ward off evil spirits or getting married when the second-hand is moving upward for good luck, many couples make superstitions an important part of their wedding day.

When the flowers get sprinkled on the way to the altar, it believed that they will bring luck for the bride and groom, either by ensuring pregnancy or simple good fortune for the couple.

When you are getting ready for the ceremony, your veil should be placed on her by a happily married woman. It's also good luck to wear your grandmother's veil of one's grandmother to assure your marriage a wealth of love from earlier generations.

Paint an egg red and place it among your decorations for good luck and prosperity.

If you drop a ring during your ceremony ask the officiant to pick it up. It's considered bad luck for the bride or groom to do so.

St. Patrick's Day is the one of the luckiest days of the year to get married. Marrying on New Year's Eve is also considered lucky as you will wake up on the first day of the new year, which is also the first day of your life together.

The wedding ring is worn on the fourth finger of your left hand since it was once believed that a vein runs from this finger to the heart.

For good luck, the groom's boutonniere is a flower from the bridal bouquet.

Making one's own wedding dress is considered bad luck. According to superstition, you will cry one tear for every stich you sew. My mother believed the same thing about sewing on Sunday.

Don't try on your entire bridal ensemble before your wedding day. Since you will want to make sure your dress fits, leaving off a shoe or glove will get around this superstition.

It is considered bad luck for a bride to sign her married name until after the ceremony. By the same token, some brides have their wedding linens embroidered with their maiden name initials instead of their married initials.

The tradition of having bridesmaids surround the bride was to confuse evil spirits.

If a bride wears pearls, she will cry during her married life because pearls means tears.

It is bad luck for a bride to read the marriage service on the day before her wedding.

It is considered bad luck for a woman to marry a man whose surname begins with the same letter as her own.

It is unlucky to marry someone born in the same month as you.

It will bring bad luck to marry on your birthday.

If it rains on the wedding day, the bride will cry all her married life. According to another superstition, it is good luck for it to rain on your wedding day.

Postponing a wedding is very bad luck.

It is bad luck for the bride to eat anything on the day before her wedding ceremony.

After you are completely dressed for the ceremony, don't look into a mirror until after you are married.

Wear earrings at your wedding and you will always be happy.

It is bad luck for your groom to see you before the ceremony.

Pearls are the symbols of tears. For each pearl that the bride wears, her husband will give her a cause for weeping.

In the saying something old, something new, the old should be something from a happily married woman, the borrowed could be a dime worn in the heel of the left shoe. "Old" expresses your connection with your past and tradition; "new" symbolizes hope for the future; "borrowed" represents the support of your family and friends (the item must be returned); "blue" exemplifies fidelity, constancy and faithfulness.

At the altar, the bride should keep her right foot ahead of the groom's.

It is unlucky to give away a wedding present.

Put a penny in your shoe for wealth in your marriage.

It is a good omen to see a rainbow on your wedding day. A black cat is equally lucky.

Let's call it Jessica's Rule: When someone falls on her butt walking into the wedding venue, it's good luck - for everyone! We made this up today when one of the guests tripped coming into the reception held at a restored train station.

To get the full value of joy
You must have someone to divide it with.

Mark Twain

CHAPTER SIX

Flowers and Their Meanings

Apple blossom – I promise

Baby's breath – celebratory, festive

Bachelor button – eager anticipation

Black-eyed Susan - faith and encouragement

Calla lily - majestic, magnificent

Camellia – gracious, benevolent, compassionate

Cosmos - peace

Daffodil – gallantry, courtliness, courtesy

Daisy - innocence

Holly – a happy home

Iris - inspiration

Ivy - faithfulness

Jasmine - elegance and grace

Lilac - young love

Magnolia - dignity

Orange blossom - fertility

Orchid - ethereal beauty

Pansy - loving thoughts

Pink carnation - gratitude

Pink rose - friendship

Pink tulip – caring, innocence

Purple tulip - royalty

Queen Anne's Lace – delicate, feminine

Red carnation - showy, sparkling

Red rose - passion, love

Red tulip – I love you

Sunflower – adoration, admiration

Sweetpea – demure, bashful

Yellow carnation - lighthearted, sunny

Yellow tulip - totally, hopelessly in love

Violet – devoted, true-blue

White carnation – loving memory

White rose - purity

Wisteria – loyal, steadfast

CHAPTER SEVEN

Centerpieces

Place whole fresh fruit or vegetables (in season, to save money) in clear glass bowls or vases. You can either have one type of fruit per bowl or mix and match, coordinating with your wedding colors. Lemons look particularly cheerful.

Small pumpkins and squash are readily available and relatively inexpensive decorations for fall weddings. If you are so inclined, you could also iron autumn leaves between wax paper. Sunflowers and wildflowers such as goldenrod (watch those allergies, though) make inexpensive bouquets to complement the autumn theme.

Tea lights inside votive holders give off a romantic and fanciful light. The holders come in many different colors and textures to match your mood. Jelly and jam containers or canning jars protect candles from wind and also display colored rocks or marbles. Freeze candles before setting them out so they will burn more slowly. If you use baby food jars, you won't have to worry if they crack and you won't have to clean them – just toss 'em. If you rub the inside bottoms with a little oil, you might be able to dig out the remains of the candles and recycle the glass.

One large glass bowl in the middle of a table with floating candles can be surrounded by flowers, votive candles, colored glass stones.

To color coordinate mismatched vases, bowls and candle holders, take empty tin cans, baby food jars, wine bottles and anything else you have outside. Put down newspaper, and spray them with primer. Let dry, then spray with your choice of color. Use these only for non-food displays.

CHAPTER EIGHT

Wedding Customs From Around The World

Want more than the traditional something old, something new, something borrowed, something blue? Honor your heritage or borrow from another culture!

Wales

Daffodil bouquets and boutonnieres - daffodils are the national flower of Wales.

Germany

Do the umbrella dance! Leave a white umbrella at the entrance to the reception, and ask guests to sign it. The umbrella is presented to you as newlyweds; hold it over your heads during your first dance while guests blow bubbles at you.

Ireland

Jumping the broom. Although a wedding broom can be purchased at ethnic stores, you may prefer to decorate a plain ol' household broom with flowers and ribbons and bows in your wedding colors.

You may jump the broom before or after your wedding ceremony.

Before: As you walk down the aisle, stop and jump the broom.

Immediately after your vows: The broom is behind you as you marry. When you turn to be presented to the guests, jump the broom before proceeding back down the aisle.

During the reception: With family and friends gathering in a circle around you, jump the broom, then dance your first dance.

A toast, prayer or blessing may be said as you jump the broom.

Greece

Since ivy is considered the symbol of eternal love, carry it in your wedding bouquet or use it in centerpieces.

Each of you could wear a crown entwined with ivy and bound together by ribbons, symbolizing the everlasting bonds of marriage.

Carry a lump of sugar in your glove on your wedding day to ensure a sweet married life.

The custom of the breaking of plates at the reception is believed to bring good luck.

Your best man swaps the rings three times between your fingers. This symbolizes the Holy Trinity.

Hebrew

At the beginning of the wedding ceremony, the bride can observe the Biblical custom of circling the groom seven times.

Jewish giving of the wedding ring: "Behold, you are betrothed unto me with this ring, according to the law of Moses and Israel."

The groom should not have money, silver articles, gold, precious stones, etc. in his pockets at the time of marriage.

To signify that a marriage is fragile and may be easily broken at the end of the ceremony or at the reception a glass is placed on the floor, and the groom shatters it with his foot. You may cover the glass with a cloth for safety's sake. This ritual also reminds us that marriage vows are as enduring as the glass is permanently shattered.

Japan

Add cherry blossoms or jasmine to your bouquet.

Fans are considered a symbol of happiness in China and Japan, so use them as table decorations or in place of bridesmaids' bouquets.

Native American

Cleanse your marriage of past evils and memories of former lovers with a purification ritual of hand washing.

Blanket Ceremony. You each are wrapped in a blue blanket, representing your pasts. After your union is blessed, remove your blue blankets so that your relatives can swaddle you in one white blanket to start your new life together.

Turquoise and silver jewelry, including rings and belts, are worn by both the bride and the groom to shield against evils including hunger, poverty and bad luck.

Scotland

Wear a horseshoe on your arm for good luck. While your maternal ancestors wore a real one, for simplicity's sake you might want to find a plastic replica.

The groom can wear a kilt.

Exchange rings with Celtic knotwork designs instead of plain gold wedding bands.

Hire a bagpiper to play during the wedding party's entrance and departure.

When leaving for your wedding, step out of the house on your right foot for luck.

Handfasting. This is from Jimmy and Bobbie's wedding.

Minister: I ask you to look into each others eyes. Will you honor and respect one another, and seek to never break that honor?

You: We will.

[the ribbon is draped over the top of the couples' hands]

Minister: Will you share each other's pain and seek to ease it?

You: We will.

[the ribbon is draped over the hands again]

Minister: Will you share the burdens of each so that your spirits may grow in this union?

You: We will.

[the ribbon is draped a third time]

Minister: Will you share each other's laughter, and look for the brightness in life and the positive in each other?

You: We will.

[the ribbon is draped the final time and tied together]

Minister: [Bride and groom], as your hands are bound together now, so your lives and spirits are joined in a union of love and trust.

Above you are the stars and below you is the earth.

Like the stars, your love should be a constant source of light, and like the earth, a firm foundation from which to grow.

[Untie the ribbon]

France

Upon pronouncing you husband and wife, your minister can place white silk over your heads. This same wrap can be kept for your child's baptism.

Canada

At your reception your unmarried siblings wear funny looking socks and dance, while your guests throw money at them (for you, of course).

Poland

An old Polish tradition is the sharing of bread, salt and wine. At the reception, the parents of the bride and groom greet the newlyweds with lightly salted bread and a glass of wine.

The bread signifies the wish of the parents that the couple will never be hungry or in need; the salt, that life may be difficult at times; the wine, the parents hope that the couple will never thirst and wish for a life of good health.

The parents then kiss the newlyweds as a sign of welcome, unity and love.

The Money Dance originated in Poland. Guests place money in an apron worn by the bride over her wedding dress. Each man must dance with the bride, and every other woman and girl at the wedding.

Hispanic – Spain, Mexico

Historically, Hispanics marry in a Catholic church by a priest. However, if that is not possible, you may add traditional touches to your DIY wedding.

Your officiant can drape an extra-long strand of rosary beads or in a white silk scarf around your shoulders after you recite your vows.

As a symbol that the groom promises to support his bride, he gives her thirteen coins in the memory of Christ and His twelve apostles. The bride carries the coins in a small bag.

A brightly colored, dancing dress with ruffles swaying at the hem is a gorgeous alternative to a white wedding gown. The groom can wear a light weight, short-sleeved shirt, otherwise known as a guayabera or wedding shirt. Your groom might want to be your matador, wearing a bolero and tight pants.

Decorate your reception hall with brightly colored flowers, tablecloths, napkins, and plates. Hang a few piñatas.

At Puerto Rican weddings, a doll dressed in a bridal gown is placed at the head table.

Serve sangria or rum and Coke, along with Mexican soda.

African

You can have your officiant or close friend tie your wrists together with a strand of cowrie or other seashells, representing prosperity and fertility, while reciting your vows.

To honor your loved ones who have recently passed away, pour water onto the ground while saying a prayer or blessing.

Jumping the broom is described in the Irish tradition section of this chapter.

To celebrate the Four Elements, you feed each other lemon (sour), vinegar (bitter), cayenne pepper (hot), and honey (sweet). This ritual demonstrates that your relationship will survive life's toughest times and then enjoy the sweetness of marriage.

Cowrie shells are often used to decorate the bridal table.

Germany

After the wedding ceremony, a German bride will give each driver a white ribbon to be tied to the radio antenna. The procession drives through town, honking. People honk back to wish them well. My brother and his wife did this years ago.

Germans wear wedding rings on their right hands. The bands are plain, without diamonds.

A German bride collects pennies for years to buy wedding shoes to make sure her marriage get off on the right foot.

Italy

Use small candles representing your individual families to light a larger candle to represent your new family.

Break a glass, and the number of pieces will represent the number of years your marriage will last.

An Italian bridegroom carries a small bit of iron in his pocket to keep the evil eye away from his wedding ceremony.

Decorate your car with fresh flowers to symbolize a new and happy life together.

Stretch a large ribbon across the doorway of the church or reception hall to signify that you are tying the knot.

Dutch

Dutch couples plant lilies of the valley in their gardens. The lily blooms each year, signifying a renewal of their love for each other.

CHAPTER TEN

Choosing Your Colors

This can be the easiest decision you make regarding your wedding.

What are you favorite colors?

What are your favorite team's colors?

Working with the seasons ensures what you want is readily available: red and green candies at Christmas, pale pink and yellow at Easter. Silver, white and blue are appropriate for New Year's Eve and winter; pastels for spring and summer; red, white and navy for Memorial Day, Fourth of July and military weddings; brown, orange and off white for all.

If your birthstones complement each other, you could consider using them as your wedding colors. If they clash, perhaps you could use lighter or darker shades until you hit on a gorgeous match.

Pick up paint chips at your local hardware or big box store and play with them to see what you like.

Aqua and watermelon are two colors that flatter most complexions. They are also young and cheery and can be used as accents.

The meaning of colors

Gold, representing wisdom and wealth, is often worn for a second marriage or by the bride's mother. It also is an excellent choice for an accent color.

Red symbolizes love, desire, joy and passion. Whether you choose candy apple, fire engine, ruby or burgundy, there is a shade of red that will showcase your beauty. Red, white, and black is a sophisticated color scheme, especially when you add a little lace to the mix. One bride wore a red satin wedding gown accented in whie while her bridesmaids' dresses were white with black sashes.

Pink is the epitome of femininity, romance and love. Magenta, rose, light pink and all shades in between suggests youth and kindness.

Brown is down to earth and stable.

Orange is associated with happiness, joy, and sunshine. Orange is invigorating, sexy and youthful. An autumn color, it is a natural with brown. For a tropical wedding (even in Minnesota in the dead of winter) team with pink, yellow, bright blue.

Yellow is warm, joyous, energetic, light hearted, and intellectually stimulating.

The color of nature, green is fresh and restful. It symbolizes spring.

Aqua is associated with emotional healing and protection.

Blue is calming, and a favorite of many men. It represents loyalty, faith and truth and in some cultures, Heaven. Since it is the color of the sky and the ocean, it is perfect for outdoor weddings, especially Native America themed celebrations.

Purple combines the stability of blue and the energy of red. Purple, associated with royalty, symbolizes nobility, luxury, wealth and ambition. Purple is associated with magic, independence, wisdom, dignity, mystery and creativity.

White is associated with innocence, purity, light and goodness. It is considered to be the color of perfection. White represents a successful beginning.

Black is a mysterious, formal and elegant color that denotes strength and authority.

Where does the family start? It starts with a young man falling in love with a girl. No superior alternative has yet been found.

Sir Winston Churchill

CHAPTER TEN

Gemstones and Birthstones

Gemstones:

If you like something other than a diamond for your ring, you might consider a gemstone. Here are a few along with their meanings.

- Amethyst is used in meditation for recovery of physical and spiritual unbalances.
- Bloodstone represents vitality and life energy.
- Moonstone is passionate and inspiring.
- Blue Lace Agate creates joy, peace and happiness.
- Carnelian represents compassion and unconditional love.
- Cherry Quartz reinforces clarity in relationships.
- Quartz Crystal can be used for communication with the spirit world, divination and scrying.
- Lapis Lazuli, embodying wisdom, is a powerful mystical stone, connecting you to Spirit Guides and the cosmic plane of existence.

- Malachite attracts money and is also a stone of spiritual wealth.
- Moss Agate represents humility. It is also a connection to the earth.
- Jade is a stone of prosperity and spiritual wealth.
- Onyx represents insight and perception.
- Red goldstone stimulates physical and spiritual energies.
- Turquoise carries powerful spiritual properties that attach themselves to the wearer. When you wear turquoise, it becomes part of you.

Birthstones:

January - garnet, rose quartz

February – amethyst, onyx

March – bloodstone

April – diamond, rock crystal

May – emerald

June – alexandrite, moonstone, pearl

July – ruby, carnelian

August – peridot

September – sapphire, lapis

October – opal

November – topaz

December – zircon, turquoise

CHAPTER ELEVEN

Theme Weddings

Destination Weddings

One couple wanting a casual yet one of a kind romantic wedding searched the Internet for historic places within driving distance from their home.   They ended up marrying in a covered bridge over a cascading waterfall with a restored grain mill in the background.   After taking their vows, they drove to a nearby metro park where they visited an authentic 1800s working farm, then hit the 2.5 mile hiking trial.   They ended the day at an decades old diner. What places of interest are within your radius?

1940's Glamourous Movie Star Wedding

The bride wore a satin slip dress such as Carole Lombard (she was well before my time, too, but I've seen pictures of her) would have worn.

She carried a bouquet of pale pink peonies and white roses, with a large white feather in the center. The groom and his men wore white feathers as boutonnieres. Although they rented a vintage mansion with gardens overflowing with old-fashioned roses, lilies and evergreens, a city park or backyard would make an excellent substitute. A bride could also have her hair done in a 20's, 30's or 40's style and dress as a flapper.

NASCAR

The easiest theme wedding was coincidental (if you believe in coincidences). The bride and groom wanted a jeans and t-shirt wedding at 8:00 a.m. on a Friday.

It was chilly that morning so I grabbed my Dale Earnhardt jacket as I left the house. "We're on our way to Bristol!" My jacket fit their wedding perfectly. This theme could be expanded to a cook-out or pizza on race day.

Baseball

Two single parents who met when their school-aged children played baseball got permission to use the ball diamond for their wedding. We all dressed up normally. I stood on home plate, with them taking their vows in front of me. Guests sat in the bleachers. The bridesmaids were on first, groomsmen on third.

Football stadium

One couple rented a college football stadium for their late morning wedding.

The bride wore a formal satin gown with a long train, a tiny college logo embroidered on the hem. Bridesmaids were also dressed in formals while the groom and his groomsmen were dressed in football jerseys. I wore a referee shirt over my customary black cocktail dress.

Guests sat in the bleachers at the 50 yard line.

The reception was held at a college area restaurant but a tailgate cook-out would also have fit this theme.

Cowboy Wedding

I've been lucky enough to be invited to participate in several country western downhome weddings.

The most elaborate had a live band, but they all were remarkably similar.

The groom wore jeans, cowboy boots, and a 10 gallon hat while the bride was dressed in a traditional white wedding gown. The groomsmen wore denim jeans.

The bridal party often wears jeans or prairie skirts. Gingham dresses also follow the theme. Decorate the bride and bridesmaid's cowboy hats with wild flowers. If cowgirl garb is too drab for you, you could always dress up as a dance hall girl, complete with petticoat and garters. Your groom could be a dandified Wyatt Earp.

Bales of hay were serving tables. Bouquets of daisies, black eyed Susans, blanket flowers, purple cornflowers and sunflowers in milk glass vases, jugs, tin juice cans and other vintage containers were everywhere. Beer and soft drinks were buried in ice-filled galvanized feeding troughs. If you don't want to spend the money for troughs, substitute the bed of a pick-up truck.

The color scheme for a cowboy wedding is easy: denim and red and white bandanas.

Old cowboy boots can be filled with a smaller vase and wildflowers.

They kept the informal theme by using paper or plastic dishes and plastic cutlery, paper napkins. Vintage mismatched dishes from thrift stores would also suit the occasion.

The menu was hearty country fare of fried chicken, cole slaw, potato salad, beef barbecue, potato chips, dip, and chili.

Accompany the wedding cake with pies, brownies and coffee.

At another country wedding the groom dug a pit and slow cooked a pig.

Southern Hospitality

No matter where you live and what your circumstances, good ol' Southern hospitality will add much to your wedding – and your marriage.

A recent reception offered barbecued meatballs, stuffed mushrooms and other delicious food. Even better than the food was the sincere question. "Did you get enough to eat?"

At another wedding, my car was filled with flat after flat of tomato plants donated to our animal rescue fundraiser. They didn't sell and since we all hate to see anything go to waste (and I am the gardener of the group), I was the designated donee.

I didn't have time to empty my car before a casual wedding a few miles away. The people were exceptionally friendly, so I decided to share my largesse with any and all who wanted a free plant or two.

One might even say I pushed the plants.

One man exclaimed, "This is just like a southern wedding!"

Have a heart that never hardens, and a temper that never tires, and a touch that never hurts.

Charles Dickens

CHAPTER TWELVE

Venues

City parks, your own back yard, historic buildings...

Many parks do not charge but do require a reservation. Some ask for a small refundable cleaning deposit and occasionally a park will be cost prohibitive for all but the most well healed.

Conservatories, mansions and museums make gorgeous backdrops for formal weddings.

Your own, or you family's, backyard can be dressed up or down for a romantic wedding, from the most casual to stately. If you plan an after dusk ceremony or reception, illuminate the pathway to your front door with solar lights.

Mesh lights make shrubs sparkle. Some of us are partial to the solar version with more subtle illumination.

VFWs and other private clubs often have a wedding arch. They are often already decorated with plastic flowers and white blinking Christmas lights, and sometimes they are a bit dusty, but they almost always photograph well.

Grange halls serve as community centers in rural areas. The one I am most familiar with is a white frame building built in the early 20th century and resembles either a church or a large one room schoolhouse. It has a basement complete with kitchen, a stage and old school chairs in the main room, and according to local brides rent is quite reasonably priced. It is so retro that it still has a rotary dial phone in the kitchen.

Wire arches can be found at garden centers. I bought mine at an outlet store for $30. It took me about three hours to put it together, but I am DIY challenged. Your groom, groomsman, father or friend could assemble this easily. Some grooms or fathers of the bride construct wedding arches from wood that become a permanent addition to their gardens.

Drape your reception hall with mini Christmas lights, blinking or solid, white or colored.

Make sure the venue you choose allows you to bring in your own food instead of requiring you to use their catering services.

CHAPTER THIRTEEN

Inexpensive Ways to Decorate the Wedding – and the Bride!

Vintage dresses and suits from any era can make beautiful wedding gowns.

Some brides get their dresses at thrift stores. One young woman proudly showed up her dress, purse and necklace that cost her $30. It fit her perfectly.

(Tip from this domestically challenged woman who learned the hard way: do not use bleach on vintage clothing as you could ruin the fabric.)

Your dress doesn't have to be white. Bridesmaids' dresses are much less expensive than wedding dresses and are available in a variety of colors.

Some brides wear prom dresses.

Think international: Sarongs, kimonos, dirndls & lederhosen. Go with your ethnic heritage or borrow someone else's. This is your day!

Jeans, boots and turquoise jewelry give a southwestern feel, and everything can be worn again and again.

A poodle skirt can be the basis for a 1950s themed wedding. Your reception can include root-beer floats, Buddy Holly music, and a 1957 Chevy getaway car. A cardboard cut-out of Elvis, James Dean, or Marilyn Monroe (or all three!) can head the reception line. Pose with them for a fun touch. [I am willing to travel to Fairmount, Indiana, where cool was born (boyhood home and burial place of James Dean) for noon weddings. However, you will have to check with the Grant County Recorder (765-668-6542) for all applicable marriage laws.]

The groom can wear a blazer or nice sweater, white shirt and dark jeans or khakis.

Ask your bridesmaids if they already have suitable dresses in their own closets. Instead of everyone buying new gowns, they could all wear dresses in the same color range. If you really love color, you could bump out the barriers and let each wear her favorite dress.

Hair jewels make a beautiful substitute for a veil. They can be found through an Internet search, or made with inexpensive "rhinestones" (available at hobby and fabric stores) attached to stick-on velcro.

For a summer wedding, consider braiding small seashells into your hair. Shells are available at craft stores for a minimal amount of money.

To continue the summery theme, larger seashells can be used to decorate place settings. You can often find an entire basket filled with seashells at dollar stores.

Other wedding favors include small bowls with M&Ms (especially nice when the seasonal colors are available) or Hershey's kisses.

Wrap plastic knives, forks & spoons in paper napkins, then tie with a ribbon, using colors that match your wedding theme.

Dollar stores often have bridal garters and white party favors suitable for weddings.

One bride's mother brought the family dogs who served as best man and maid of honor. Corsages, from a dollar store, were wired onto their collars.

If you can't afford armloads of fresh flowers, or you are allergic, here are a few suggestions for your beautiful wedding:

In spring and summer, varieties of purple wildflowers in shades from light to dark grow at roadsides. At the first part of July, native or "tiger" lilies appear to flourish in every ditch in Ohio.

Candles are the easiest and most affordable alternative to flowers.

Tea lights, available from a dollar store, can float in a punch bowl or individual glasses. Buy glasses at dollar stores, yard sales, thrift stores, and flea markets.

A large candle held in place with clear or colored stones makes a beautiful centerpiece.

Use a candle surrounded by clear bowls or glasses filled with cranberries and pine boughs for a Christmas wedding.

Know anyone with a classic car? A vintage Mustang, Barracuda, or convertible will make a great "limo" for your wedding day.

Consider hiring an art student as your official wedding photographer, if you want to get formal. Family and friends can be counted on to take digital pictures.

Cupcakes, Twinkies, snowballs, or several flavors of pie can be substituted for or an addition to the wedding cake.

Potted herbs are a beautiful and refreshing decoration.

Scarves in your wedding colors can be wrapped around bowls.

Potted bulbs in season can be used to decorate.

Unity Candles

Symbolizing two individuals becoming one, unity candles may be lighted immediately upon walking up the aisle, while a friend or sister recites a poem, your minister reads a blessing, after you say your vows or during your wedding reception.

Your mothers and any children of the bride or groom may also participate by light the unity candle. This is a wonderful way to unite a family.

Some couples relight the unity candle on their anniversary.

Unity Sand

You don't have to marry on a beach to add a unity sand ceremony to your wedding. A sand ceremony is for everyone!

If you are marrying on a beach, grab some sand! You also might have collected sand and kept it from a special vacation. However, for most of us, it is more practical to buy sand. Sand ceremony kits are available on the Internet, or you can do it yourself.

Aside from the sand (which you can buy at a craft store or pet shop), you will need one large vase and two smaller pouring vases. White is traditional, but the bride and groom can each have their own colored sand.

The groom first pours some of the sand into the unity vase, then the bride and groom alternate, layering the sand. Both pour what is left from their vases at the same time, filling the vase.

While pouring the sand, the bride and groom may repeat a blessing or the officiant may read a poem or prayer of the couple's choosing.

Unity Stones

Substitute colored glass or stones for the sand. These are available at dollar stores and craft shops.

Guest Book

Place a blank book on each table entitled, "The Most Important Things to Remember About Marriage" and ask guests to leave a message and sign it. You can have a book made online, or buy plain guest books at dollar stores and print out the title on clear plastic labels to affix on the front.

Use your imagination, and enjoy your day!!!

CHAPTER FOURTEEN

Green Wedding Favors

Here are a few ideas for environmentally friendly wedding favors.

If you marry in September, October or November, you can place two or three spring flowering bulbs such as daffodils or tulips in a net bag, tie with color coordinated ribbons and give to each guest, along with simple instructions. (Example: "Daffodils. Plant in autumn six inches deep. Allow foliage to die back after flowering each spring before mowing.")

In spring or winter, flower seeds are a cheerful favor, along with summer flowering bulbs such as stargazer lilies, dahlias, hardy gladiolus, or cannas.

Cuttings from your garden placed in small water filled vases or bottles are a beautiful way to share your Wedding of the Century.

Tree seedlings can be purchased for $1 each or less (look on online for a supplier), planted in peat moss or potting soil, watered lightly, and put in sandwich bags with twist ties topped with colored ribbons to keep everything neat. These also make great favors for wedding anniversaries and birthdays.

CHAPTER FIFTEEN

Inexpensive Alternatives to Traditional Wedding Cakes

Here are a few ideas that might help you save money on your wedding:

Use a small decorated cake for wedding pictures, and serve guests from a plain sheet cake.

Sprinkle the top of a cake (store-bought or home baked) with edible (repeat, EDIBLE) flowers, candied or *au naturel*. In springtime, ever-romantic violets are everywhere. Do not use any flowers that have been exposed to pesticides, and even though they are edible, use for decorative purposes only. Don't eat them.

To candy flower petals, beat one egg white until foamy. Dip small brush into egg white, then paint flowers. Sprinkle lightly with superfine sugar; allow to dry (usually 24 hours).

Get wedding favors from dollar and craft stores. Put a small plastic champagne glass filled with flower sprinkles or chocolate hearts on top of iced cake, then circle with silver balls. You can also place red or pink sprinkles in heart shapes over top.

If you know by February 14 that you are getting married, you can get your reception favors on Valentine's Day clearance. This past year I picked up heart shaped full sized plastic plates, red, of course, for 37 cents each, along with a package of twelve red doilies for 41 cents. Since I didn't have any use for boxes of pink rose petals - not that I needed the plates or doilies - I didn't purchase them at 75% off $2.

Your wedding cake doesn't have to be decorated with hearts and flowers. One couple bought a cake, decorated with elephants, at the grocery store. They like elephants, so this was their choice for their wedding day.

Want something different? Substitute pie. Cheesecake, cookies, doughnuts are also good alternatives.

One couple arranged Twinkies, snowballs and brownies on a cake pedestal. Another's teen-aged sister baked the cake and cupcakes in heart shaped pans, frosting the cake with white icing, the cupcakes with pink.

For the ultimate two for the price of one, how about a white pizza? You can cut it like cake, yet serve it for the wedding dinner.

—

CHAPTER SIXTEEN

Reception Recipes

Punch Bowl Ice Ring

Layer cherries and juice or punch a few inches; freeze; add another layer; freeze. Your punch won't get diluted as the ring melts.

Orange Punch

2 – 2 liter bottles orange soda

1 quart orange sherbert

Two cups gin, if desired

Put ice ring in punch bowl. Pour in dry orange soda and gin; gently stir in orange.

Mint Flavored Base for Lemonade or Punch

1 cup fresh mint and/or lemon balm

3 cups water

1 cup sugar

Heat water until it begins to boil. Place mint in a glass jar or bowl; add water; cover with lid and let steep for at least one hour or overnight. Strain the brew; refrigerate. Add as a base for lemonade or cocktails.

Sangria

1 bottle of red wine, chilled

1 each lemon, lime and orange, cut into slices

2 Tablespoons sugar

1/4 cup orange juice

1 cup strawberries, raspberries or strawberries, fresh or frozen

1 can diced pineapples

4 cups ginger ale

Pour wine into a large pitcher; squeeze the juice from the citrus slices into the wine.

Add fruit slices and pineapple. Stir in sugar and orange juice. Add ginger ale, berries and ice just before serving.

Chocolate Dessert Cups

Melt a bag of chocolate chips in microwave, then pour several Tablespoons into foil or paper muffin wrappers you placed in a muffin pan for support. Spread on the bottom and up the sides of wrappers. Refrigerate until hardened; peel wrappers; fill chocolate cups with ice cream, cooled pudding, fruit.

Chocolate Pretzels

One 9 oz. package of melting chocolate

One bag pretzels

Sprinkles

Nuke melting chocolate using package directions. Dip one end of pretzel half-way or a third of the way up, shake or scrape off excess. If you are like me, you will like having the extra chocolate and won't bother removing a drop. Sprinkle with baking sprinkles; you can choose red and green for Christmas; orange for Hallowe'en, etc. Place on parchment, aluminum foil or waxed paper and refrigerate for 30 minutes to make sure the chocolate is set. Store in covered container in refrigerator.

Honey Strawberries

Dip fresh strawberries in honey, then lightly sprinkle with red pepper flakes.

Wedding Punch

1 can pineapple juice

1 quart sherbert

1 quart vanilla ice cream

1 2 liter bottle ginger ale or 7 up

Combine pineapple juice, sherbert and ice cream. Stir until smooth. Add 7 up or ginger ale. Serve immediately.

Fancy (yet easy) Bombe

1 carton mint chocolate chip (or any other) ice cream

1 package chocolate chips

Chopped nuts

Remove carton from ice cream, place on attractive serving plate; refreeze. Melt chocolate chips, pour over top of ice cream; refreeze. Immediately before serving, sprinkle with chopped nuts.

Fondue

Fondue is inexpensive yet elegant. All you need are a few different fondue pots with sauces like cheese, broth, marshmallow and chocolate. Serve foods to dip into the fondue, such as meat cut into chunks or strips, bread broken in pieces or chunks, fruits, veggies and candy. Then everyone can chat, dip and eat.

Chocolate Fondue

One can chocolate frosting

1/4 cup evaporated milk, sweetened condensed milk, or whole milk (you need something to dilute the frosting)

One tablespoon butter, if desired

Optional: 2 tablespoons orange juice or any extract including vanilla, almond, peppermint

Nuke one minute, stir, continue microwaving another minute. Stir until well blended. Pour into heated serving bowl and serve with banana slices, strawberries, or other fruit, and inch squares of pound or angel food cake.

A chocolate fountain is a romantic alternative to fondue. Graham crackers, marshmallows, orange slices, and strawberries are luscious drenched in chocolate.

Sausage Balls

1 pound sausage

2 cups biscuit mix

8 to 10 ounces shredded sharp cheese

finely chopped onions and garlic (optional)

fresh or dried oregano (optional)

Mix ingredients well, shape into balls, and bake in a preheated 400 degree oven until brown.

Tomato Salad

Cut top from tomatoes; spread with cream cheese; sprinkle with chives, oregano, or basil, or all three!

Mexican Coffee

Into each cup of coffee, substitute an equal amount of brown sugar for granulated, then add 1/4 teaspoon cinnamon or stir coffee with a cinnamon stick.

Festive Hot Chocolate

Stirring hot chocolate with a cinnamon stick is always festive and tasty. Candy canes are great at the holidays.

Pork Barbecue

Marinate pork in apple juice, then cover with barbecue sauce and bake in oven or crockpot. You can cut the sauce with an equal amount of catsup if barbecue sauce is too tangy for your tastes.

Chili is inexpensive to make and easy to prepare. Brown hamburger, drain the grease. Add chili beans, tomato sauce and chili seasonings. Mix thoroughly and allow the chili to simmer, stirring occasionally. Make it ahead, put it into a slow cooker and serve with sour cream, grated cheese, minced onions and crackers.

Lasagna and garlic bread are also hearty. Make it yourself or buy it frozen.

A spiral ham and a large pan of macaroni and cheese will feed a crowd. Serve with mustard, pickles, cherry tomatoes and onions.

Deviled eggs

2 dozen large eggs
3 Tablespoons apple or white cider vinegar
3 Tablespoons Miracle Whip salad dressing

1 Tablespoon ordinary yellow mustard

2 Tablespoons sugar

Paprika

Hard cook two dozen eggs. Drain, rinse in cool water, crack shells open, cut in half lengthwise, remove yolks and put into a separate bowl.

Mash yolks, moisten with vinegar. Mix in Miracle Whip, sugar and yellow mustard. Fill egg white halves with mixture, cover and refrigerate three hours. Sprinkle with paprika shortly before serving. Always keep deviled eggs refrigerated or well chilled (inside a cooler filled with ice).

Barbecued Meatballs

2 packages frozen meatballs

2 bottles your favorite brand barbecue sauce

1 can root beer (optional)

Cook in slow cooker; after meatballs are cooked through, turn down to low.

Pigs in blankets are a favorite. Wrap hot dogs in crescent rolls; bake.

If you have leftovers, you can always send them home with your guests or arrange beforehand to donate them to a homeless shelter.

Love never claims, it ever gives.

Mohandas K. Gandhi

CHAPTER SEVENTEEN

Wedding Checklist

Congratulations! You're getting married! Now what do you do?

- Set your date, time and location.
- Reserve church and reception hall.
- What kind of wedding do you want?
  - Formal? Casual? At home?
  - Outdoor? Afternoon or evening?
  - Religious or civil?
- Your vows
- Book your wedding officiant.
  - The absolute most important thing to remember is to confirm the date and time with your officiant as early as possible, then call to confirm two or three days before the wedding.

- o Computer glitches and other unforeseen events can cause a calamity. Always give your minister a cell number in case of an emergency. If you change your phone number, please make sure your officiant has the new number.
- Choose your colors.
- Choose bridesmaids and groomsmen, including ushers.
- Theme weddings are fun and guarantee a unique Day of Days.
- If you, the bride, will be given away, your father, step-father or both, or both your parents, your children or anyone you wish to honor may walk you down the aisle.
- "Who giveth this woman in marriage?" may be answered by your father as "I do" or "her mother and I do."
- Compile your guest list.
- Select florist, musician, photographer/videographer and caterer. Local colleges can give you names of talented photographers and caterers.
- Select your wedding dress, veil, shoes.
- Select bridesmaids' dresses.
- Select groom's and groomsmen's tuxedos.
- Select wedding cake.
- Create invitations.

Two to four weeks before the wedding

- Apply for marriage license.
- Confirm everything -- church, reception site, minister, florist, musician, photographer, videographer and caterer.

Two souls with but a single thought, two hearts that beat as one.

Friedrich Halm

CHAPTER EIGHTEEN

Your Wedding Budget

- Invitations and announcements
- Wedding rings
- Music
- Fees: organist, minister, venue (church, reception hall)
- Flowers
- Bridal and bridesmaids' bouquets' for the bride and bridesmaids
- Groomsmen's boutonnieres
- Mothers' and grandmothers' corsages
- Presents to bridesmaids and groomsmen

- Reception: food, candles, flowers

- Honeymoon

Love would never be a promise of a rose garden unless it is showered with light of faith, water of sincerity and air of passion.

Anonymous

CHAPTER NINETEEN

The Processional

This is a simple matter, based on common sense and courtesy.

When the guests arrive for a wedding the ushers seat them.

Traditionally, friends and family sit on the bride's or groom's side. However, it is a cordial gesture when guests sit on the "other side" when either the bride or groom is under represented due to family circumstances.

The closer the relationship your guests have to you, the further up front they sit.

The groom and his best man wait inside the church for the arrival of the bride and her party.

Immediately before the ceremony, the ushers escort the grandparents of the bride and groom to their seats.

Then the ushers escort the mother of the groom and mother of the bride to their seats. The mother of the bride is the last person seated.

The bridesmaids are escorted by the groomsmen.

The maid or matron of honor is escorted by the best man.

The ringbearer and flower girl walk down the aisle.

You, the bride, are escorted by your father, brother, both parents, or you may walk by yourself or with your groom.

If you desire, the officiant asks, "Who giveth this woman in marriage?" to which your father answers, "I do" or "Her mother and I do."

You exchange vows.

After the wedding ceremony, you accompany the minister to a quiet spot to have the wedding certificate signed.

Guests blow bubbles at the newlyweds for good luck.

Your photographer takes pictures of you leaving the church.

CHAPTER TWENTY

Questions and Answers

Answers to questions asked by prospective brides.

Q.   Could you marry us without a marriage license?

A.   If you want a legal marriage, you must have a license.

Q.   Can't we just tell people we're married? Isn't that what common law marriage is?

A.   Common law marriages are legal in only a few states. For your own protection, including health and life insurance, it is worth the effort to obtain a marriage license and your relationship authenticated and sanctioned by a minister, judge or other officiant recognized by the government.   Common law came from the days when people lived out in the sticks and couldn't get to a preacher or a circuit rider only came through occasionally.

Q.   How did people get married in Biblical times? Didn't they just announce they were together?

A.   We are living in modern times and must abide by current laws in order to protect our families.

Q.   Is pre-marital sex wrong? We have already have been together but should we wait until we get married?

A.   Pre-marital sex is not the same as adultery, unless you are married to someone else. If you have already had sex with your intended, it might make your wedding night more special if you remain celibate from your engagement until your marriage.

Q.   What is the purpose of blood tests?

A.   The purpose of blood tests is to detect serious communicable disease, primarily syphilis. Blood tests originated in the 1930s in the days before penicillin and other antibiotics. Although they haven't been used in Ohio for years, blood tests are mandatory in a handful of states. Run an Internet search for "marriage laws" to find out if blood tests or waiting periods apply to your situation.

Q.   Why can't we have a commitment ceremony instead of getting a marriage license?

A.   You may have a commitment ceremony, but it is not legally binding. There are valid reasons for having a commitment ceremony. In many states since same sex marriage is not legal, couples may instead make their vows to love and care for each other.

One couple who had dated for a month before moving in together weren't ready for a legal marriage but wanted a ceremony for their young children's sake.

One older woman wanted to retain her widow's pension but live as husband and wife after being reunited with her first love.

Q.   If I change my mind after you sign the license, can you cancel the marriage?

A.   One person asked me this before booking me (what odds would you give that marriage?) and another called the evening after her small home wedding. Her mother-in-law sat in a chair up front and picked at the bride both before and after the ceremony. The criticism was particularly nasty, aimed at the bride's weight (she looked normal to me) as well as her housekeeping and mothering skills (again, more than adequate).

Once the minister signs the license and returns it to the court (usually by mail), you are legally married.

Q.   I know it used to be part of the ceremony, but do we have to have "obey" as part of our vows?

A.   This is an archaic term, and I personally would never marry someone who wanted to use it. Marriage is between equals, and "obeying" sounds like it means the husband can control (or even abuse) his wife.

Q.   How long after the death of a parent or grandparent should a couple wait to get married? What if all the details of the wedding have already been established and confirmed?   May we go ahead?

A.   This is a time to use sensitivity along with common sense. If you are up to a wedding, the joy of the day could help relieve your grief.   If a parent lost a spouse and doesn't feel she or he can enjoy your day and it is possible to postpone without losing deposits, you could have a quiet ceremony now, and a celebration later.

You could also have a member of the party read a poem in honor of your loved one, and leave a a single flower or bouquet on a chair at the altar or at a reception table. It is not disrespectful for you to go on with your life and in fact is a testament of the spirit, gift and power that love bestows on all of us.

Q.   I think covered bridges are romantic, but what are they for?

A.   A hundred years ago and more, covered bridges sheltered horses and buggies during rain. This means you can have an outdoor wedding rain or shine or even snow.

CHAPTER TWENTY-ONE

Renewal of Vows

Congratulations! Your marriage is a success! If anyone deserves a gala, it is you.

Play a song the year you were married.

"Her name was Lola..." as you two lovebirds amaze your kids (and perhaps grandkids) by dancing in a conga line.

Were you married in the 1960s? Straight hair for the girls, Beatle haircuts for the guys. Not enough hair left? How about a Summer of Love theme? Daisies are inexpensive.

Were you married in the 1970s? Disco outfits? Bee Gees?

The 1980s? Big hair!

A fun way to exchange your renewals could be at an old car show. Or rent a vintage automobile and drive off into the sunset of your second honeymoon.

A hot hair balloon ride is a fanciful way to keep romance alive.

CHAPTER TWENTY-TWO

Memorable Weddings

One wedding scheduled for a secluded spot – given the choice of a park where a few people might be picnicking and one that usually is deserted, a couple chose the isolated site – almost didn't come off.

When the groom pulled up in his SUV, alone, I waited.

As he started walking to a covered bridge, he said, "She's in the back seat. Tell her we're here."

Quite tentatively, if not actually frightened, I walked up to the SUV and looked through the back window.

I didn't see anyone.

"She's lying down. She's under the sheet."

Now I was afraid. What had I gotten myself into? I could make a run for my car, and if I made it, lock the doors and see how fast my car could go from zero to sixty.

Scenes from *Psycho* ran through my head, then images of *Mary Jane's Last Dance*.

He wanted to marry a dead woman?

Was she "merely" dead or had she been murdered? Was she mummified? Was there ever a bride, living or dead? How crazy was he? Was my life in danger?

He opened the door and the bride, dressed beautifully in a white satin gown, sat up. She was even wearing a veil.

"I wasn't supposed to see her in her wedding dress yet." She dressed and gotten into their vehicle without him seeing her. The plan was for him to walk to the covered bridge, and keep his back turned until she walked up the aisle.

After the wedding, I confessed my fears.

They were decent, spiritually motivated people and we laughed about the misunderstanding.

Another wedding was not so dramatic, but unforgettable just the same. The groom aka Prince Charming, dressed in a blue jacket with fringed gold epaulettes on the shoulders, gold belt, and brown pants with gold side stripe, met me at the gazebo as we waited for his bride aka Cinderella. She wore a white sleeveless dress, white opera length gloves, a blue headband, and black choker necklace. It was cute, and they lived happily ever after. Unfortunately, I had to leave before the reception was over and drive directly to a Jewish funeral, the first (and so far, only) one I've ever attended.

The three day from proposal to altar wedding was one I'll never forget, mainly because it was flawless. The bride wore a white gown, a prom dress purchased off the rack at the mall, the ceremony was in the patio of the restaurant where the couple had their first date, we dined on white pizza, and drank samples of wine. They decided on a Monday to get married, got their license, bought rings, made their reservation at the restaurant and booked me on Tuesday, and wed on Wednesday. There was nothing rushed or hurried about the ceremony.

The most memorable wedding was one I was unable to attend, four hours north in Lake Erie. "In" Lake Erie, not by. The bride's brother was ordained but didn't realize he had to register with the secretary of state's office before he could perform a legal wedding ceremony. The bride called two days before the wedding, but not only could I not drive four hours each way, I was already booked for two weddings.

My suggestions? Call the local probate court and get phone numbers of ministers, or search online (but that's how she found me, and only me), or ... this is a little off the wall, but would you consider having your brother conduct the ceremony, realizing it isn't legal, and then drive down to meet me a day or two later so I marry you? We could meet somewhere, I could ask you if you "do" and sign your license. The bride liked the idea and we met two days after the wedding. She showed me digital pictures of her and the groom standing off the shore, in the water, of Lake Erie. They had the wedding of their dreams and I didn't have to drive eight hours.

As the bride walked down the aisle, one of my favorite songs, "You Raise Me Up," played. You might be thinking that everyone likes "You Raise Me Up." While that may be true, how many people also like or are even familiar with   "It's Good to Be Us?" Bucky Covington led the bridal party back down the white carpet and into the reception. Not Bucky Covington in the flesh! It was a recording. Had Bucky showed up, this would have been the most memorable wedding of my career.

A young man spoke broken English, his bride none. From what I could make out, they wanted to get married, immediately, and they had their license. I drove to a local grocery store parking lot and with our cars facing each other married them by headlights at 9:00 p.m. They had already married in North Carolina but it was a Catholic ceremony. I couldn't make myself understood so cheerfully asked them if they took each other in marriage. I wondered if they thought they needed to get married in each state where they live or if they didn't understand that in America a marriage is a marriage, whether religious or civil.

As you know in some countries, a legal ceremony must precede a religious one in order for the marriage to be valid. What I remember is the young bride's innocence and bravery. It would be so difficult to come to the U.S. and leave family behind, and not even be able to speak English.

Raggedy Ann and Raggedy Andy were united in holy matrimony on Halloween with a weinie roast following the nuptials.

I often wonder about the fate of the nineteen year olds dressed in Army fatigues on the way for their boots to hit the ground. They were so young and innocent – and cute. Although I've married several grooms on their way to A Foreign Land, this was the first couple who were both enlisted in the Armed Services.

One groom I knew only from a grocery store where he works. During football season he wears a scarlet and gray fright wig, so you can imagine my shock at seeing him alighting from a limo dressed in a tuxedo.

One Sunday morning as I was coloring my hair, I received a phone call from a couple wanting a last minute wedding. Although they had called several weeks earlier to inquire about my fee, they had never gotten back to confirm. They were in my lane!

I rinsed out the dye, wrapped my hair, put on a dress and ran out to meet them. Professional people (veterinarians), this was the only time they had. They were casually dressed, so they didn't mind being married by a woman with a beach towel on her head.

Over the years two brides were excited that both they and the minister were pregnant. My waistline and midriff aren't what they used to be, and they were embarrassed when I told them I was not.

I was flattered to think that considered me in their general age group and a little sad that my baby making days are firmly in the past.

———

After conducting a prison wedding, I was unnerved when a sentinel refused to unlock the door and allow us to exit the visiting area. Although the chaplain rang the buzzer several times, the guard in charge ignored us. The custodian assigned to the groom commented, "She's in a snit today."

One young bride's sister, still needing a carrier to help her sit up, was escorted into the wedding in a little red wagon, festooned with ribbons.

Another bride read a tender letter to her daddy who had died a few years earlier. She told him how much she still loved and missed him, and thanked him for all the things he had taught her. She introduced him to her groom and asked for his blessing for their marriage.

While it is tradition to leave a white rose on a chair to honor a deceased parent or grandparent, one bride left a bright colored hibiscus in memory of her mother. I personally would love to cheerful flowers replace the white rose.

A bride, widowed with grown children, was reunited with a boy she had dated in high school. They had a wedding in a daughter's living room, with kittens rolling around on the floor, playing with my feet.

At one wedding, the couple's golden retriever stood beside the groom to serve as best man. I don't know if he threw a bachelor party the night before, but would guess he didn't.

Two rescued doggies showed up at an outdoor wedding wearing crepe paper boutonnieres from a dollar store wired to their collars.

One summer afternoon at a casual wedding in a city park gazebo, a plump black cat strolled up before the ceremony and stayed, and then a butterfly landed on my hand and also stayed. It was particularly poignant or uplifting, depending upon how you look at it, since the wedding occurred on my late husband's birthday.

One morning a man called to request a last minute wedding, giving only his first name, a very common one. Even though I never ask personal questions (what I don't know I cannot repeat), I did ask him his age.

"Thirty-six." "I think you went to school with my son. Did you graduate from Lancaster High School?" No, he was home schooled from the ninth grade on, because he was shot on the bus. He and my son indeed rode the same bus, but my son stayed home sick that day. When I heard about it on the news, I was working thirty miles away at a new job and didn't feel I could drive home, but I called home just to make sure he had stayed home. The victim was shot in the spine and not expected to walk ever again.

———

I hadn't thought about this in years, but cried when the groom told me that his grandfather took him to church and people prayed over him.

He also got it into his head that the doctors were wrong. I thought perhaps the groom would limp, but instead hopped out of his SUV along with his wife.

"Are you Miracle Man?" Indeed he was. Marrying him was an honor.

At a rural wedding, a brindle pit bull showed up and sniffed me.

After the ceremony, the groom asked me whose dog it was. "Some boys were playing in the creek. It's probably theirs. A dog showing up at a wedding is good luck!"

The couple had never heard that particular superstition. There's a reason for that. I just made it up. (And that's how superstitions are born.)

After one wedding, the groom presented me with a bouquet of pink carnations and baby's breath.

One of the most unusual weddings was conducted at the ruins at Old Zion Cemetery a county east of where I live. It was the type of wedding I had wanted to perform for years.

The one room church, complete with pot-belled stove, has been gone for several years. Many of the groom's ancestors including his father are buried there and a cousin of the groom's wedding was one of the last performed in the church. The groom and his lovely bride exchanged vows on the sandstone steps.

After the ceremony the bride whispered and pointed out a shy guest cuddled up against what was left of the foundation. A baby rabbit had been there during the entire ceremony. The couple had chosen full religious rites since it was an outdoor church wedding, and it was longer than a civil service. Call me superstitious, but I believe Bunny was a representative of family members able to attend in spirit only.

This past fall, a prospective bride asked my availability for a Halloween wedding. It was a Monday, so I would be free at my lunch hour if they wanted to drive to me or any time after work. Then ... since it's Halloween would I be willing to conduct the service in a cemetery? Yes, as long as it is during daylight and not satanic.

Did I have any suggestions for the venue? If they were able to drive to Columbus, we conduct the ceremony in front of landmark monument honoring a little boy with a lifelike statute. Little Georgie died over 100 years ago when he fell at his father's hotel.

Any place else? How about the graveyard where my ancestors lie? We could marry near a Revolutionary War veteran or three year old "Sweet Caroline," a child whose birth name is similar to mine and either great-great, etc. aunt or cousin "x" times removed.

At dusk, the groom (dressed in black dress slacks and white shirt with a white boutinneire) and the bride (black dress and carrying white roses) exchanged solemn vows next to the grave of Caroline Alspach.

It's not important, but the couple was not Goth.

As we drove off, I noticed a rainbow stretched across the sky above the entire cemetery.

Two memorable weddings occurred within a week of each other. The first one was a ninety minute drive through the green belt, ending up at a lovingly maintained farm house, complete with a front porch and two swings. An hand-built arch, decorated with yellow ribbon and daisies was attached to the bottom of the steps. A German shepherd fitted with a matching bow mingled with the guests, as did her boyfriend. His hind quarters might have been paralyzed and he might have had to drag himself around, but guys will be guys. His girlfriend was in heat, and he tried his best to accommodate her. The bridal party assured us that he was in no pain (he didn't appear to be) and a doggy walker was on order.

A few days later, when I pulled up to the covered bridge where I conduct a good percentage of my weddings, I was startled to see cherry tops flashing on three - count 'em, three - cruisers. I called the bride's cell and learned that she and her fiance were quite the sports and the show would go on regardless. They were fifteen minutes out, so I waited awhile before getting out of my car. One deputy walked over and told me this was private property (it isn't), that I needed permission from the owner to conduct a wedding, and that I was interfering with a crime scene. Could I marry them at the side of the road? It is closed to through traffic. No. I have to have permission from the "owner." A guest got out of her car and quick thinker that she is stated that she was sure the bride had called ahead for permission.

When I asked - twice; I'm a slow learner - what was going on I was told this was a crime scene.

A teen-ager had parked his car and threatened to jump off the bridge. He was already cuffed and stuffed and on his way to be delivered to his parents at their home.

After the deputies departed, we walked over to the "crime scene" and the couple got hitched without a hitch.

The next week, I performed a last minute ceremony at the covered bridge early on a Friday morning. The groom handed me the license before the couple took their vows. I must have had a puzzled look on his face because he said, "Is everything all right with the license?"

The license was fine. The bride and I shared a most unusual maiden name, Alspaugh. "We're related. But more interesting than that - do you realize our family owned this property years ago?"

Two hundred and thirty five years after our common ancestor fought in the Revolutionary War and settled in Fairfield County, Ohio, his eighth generation granddaughter was married by his seventh generation granddaughter, neither of whom realized the other existed.

I traveled back a long dirt lane, past restored collectible farm equipment, the name of which I'd never heard before: Cockshutt, to marry a couple before their friends in family in front of a pond filled with bluegills and trout. The groom and his men wore vests made out of hunting camouflage material with bright orange lapels. The bridesmaids wore dresses made of the same material, with matching orange gussets.

A hound and pit bull, after sniffing my dog and cat scented shoes, circled me, then stood beside us during the ceremony. Outdoors, dogs, ponds, and a religious ceremony -- what a lovely way to commit to a life together.

One wedding was memorable because one of the mothers was from California (and wanted everyone to know it), was well to do or at least expensively dressed (I can't afford such clothing, but I know it when I see it), and may I add snobbish. When I got to the reception hall, I said hi, as I always do, and she ignored me. After the patio wedding, we returned to the hall, where she stopped me and said, "I'm sorry I didn't speak to you. I thought you were the help." As a hired gun, not an invited guest - have Bible, will travel - I am "the help." Since I was wearing a black cocktail dress and heels along with full make-up, let's assume she didn't expect a minister to be a woman.   The food was excellent thanks to the hard working, creative and talented "help." I made two passes through the food line, and was very thankful on behalf of the bride that her new mother-in-law lived 2,000 miles away.

Another mother-in-law sat in an easy chair in the couple's living room and criticized the bride (her weight, her mothering and housekeeping abilities), right through the ceremony. For a moment I thought my own dear *Schwiegermutter* had returned from the other side. Fortunately, I had another commitment and was not able to stay for the reception.

—

My latest memorable wedding took place in a former bank dating from the 1920s, and in recent decades covered over and used as office space. Now restored, this facility, with chandelier and arching windows, features the old vault as the bar area. The bride and groom recreated a Renaissance theme. *Little Red Riding Hood* played when the bridal party descended the steps to be introduced.

Life without love is meaningless and goodness without love is impossible.

Greg Jurkiewicz

CHAPTER TWENTY-THREE

Sample Ceremonies

Christian – Any Denomination

We are gathered here to witness and to celebrate the joining of this man, _____, and this woman, _____, in holy matrimony. Marriage is not to be entered into lightly, but rather undertaken with great consideration and respect for both the other person and oneself.

A reading from 1 Corinithian 13:4-13

Love is patient, love is kind. It does not envy, it does not boast, it is not proud. It is not rude, it is not self-seeking, it is not easily angered, it keeps no record of wrongs.

Love does not delight in evil but rejoices with the truth. It always protects, always trusts, always hopes, always perseveres. Love never fails.

But where there are prophecies, they will cease; where there are tongues, they will be stilled; where there is knowledge, it will pass away. For we know in part and we prophesy in part, but when perfection comes, the imperfect disappears. When I was a child, I talked like a child, I thought like a child, I reasoned like a child. When I became a man, I put childish ways behind me. Now we see but a poor reflection as in a mirror; then we shall see face to face. Now I know in part; then I shall know fully, even as I am fully known. And now these three remain: faith, hope and love. But the greatest of these is love.

Intent:

[Groom], will you have this woman to be your wedded wife, to live together in holy matrimony? Will you love her, comfort her, honor and keep her in sickness and in health, in sorrow and in joy, and forsaking all others, be faithful to her as long as you both shall live?

[Groom]: I do.

[Bride], will you have this man to be your wedded husband, to live together in holy matrimony? Will you love him, comfort him, honor and keep him in sickness and in health, in sorrow and in joy, and forsaking all others, be faithful to him as long as you both shall live?
[Bride]: I do.

Reading by groom's sister (or anyone else you choose):
By the power that Christ brought from heaven,
mayst thou love me.
As the sun follows its course,
mayst thou follow me.
As light to the eye,
as bread to the hungry,
as joy to the heart,
may thy presence be with me,
oh one that I love,
'til death comes to part us asunder.

Vows:

I, [Groom], take you, [Bride], for my lawful wife, to have and to hold, from this day forward, for better, for worse, for richer, for poorer, in sickness and health, until death do us part.

I, [Bride], take you, [Groom], for my lawful husband, to have and to hold, from this day forward, for better, for worse, for richer, for poorer, in sickness and health, until death do us part.

The Blessing of the Rings:

The wedding ring is the outward and visible sign of an inward and spiritual bond which unites two loyal hearts in endless love. It is a seal of the vows [Groom] and [Bride] have made to one another. Bless, Oh God these rings, that [Groom] and [Bride], who give them, and who wear them, may ever abide in thy peace, living together in unity, love and happiness for the rest of their lives

The Exchange of Rings:

[Groom], [Bride], I give you this ring as a symbol of our vows, and with all that I am, and all that I have, I honor you. In the name of the Father, and of the Son, and of the Holy Spirit, with this ring, I thee wed.

[Bride]: [Groom], I give you this ring as a symbol of our vows, and with all that I am, and all that I have, I honor you. In the name of the Father, and of the Son, and of the Holy Spirit, with this ring, I thee wed.

Our Father who art in heaven,
Hallowed be thy name,
Thy kingdom come,
Thy will be done in earth, as it is in heaven.
Give us this day our daily bread.
And forgive us our trespasses,
as we forgive those who trespass against us.

And lead us not into temptation,

but deliver us from evil:

For thine is the kingdom,

and the power, and the glory,

for ever. Amen.

Declaration of Marriage: In as much as you have each pledged to the other your lifelong commitment, love and devotion, I now pronounce you husband and wife.

Matthew 19:6 - So they are no longer two, but one. Therefore what God has joined together, let no one put asunder.

[Groom], you may kiss your bride!

The Lord bless and keep you; the Lord make His light to shine upon you. The Lord lift up His countenance and give you peace. Amen.

Civil

We are gathered here to celebrate the joining of this man, [Groom], and this woman, [Bride], in holy matrimony.

Marriage is not to be entered into lightly, but rather undertaken with great consideration and respect for both the other person and oneself.

Intent:

[Groom], do you take [Bride] to be your wife, to share the good times and the bad, side by side? Do you give her your hand and heart, as you pledge your faith and love?

(I do)

[Bride], do you take [Groom] to be your husband, to share the good times and the bad, side by side? Do you give you him your hand and heart, as you pledge your faith and love?

(I do)

Navajo Wedding Blessing

Now you have lit a fire and that fire should not go out.

The two of you now have a fire that represents love, understanding and a philosophy of life.

It will give you heat, food, warmth and happiness.

The new fire represents a new beginning - a new life and a new family.

The fire should keep burning; you should stay together.

You have lit the fire for life, until old age separates you.

Vows:

I, [Groom] , take you, [Bride], to be my beloved wife, to have and to hold , to honor you, to treasure you, to be at your side in sorrow and in joy, in the good times, and in the bad, and to love and cherish you always. I promise you this from my heart, for all the days of my life.

I, [Bride], take you, [Groom], to be my beloved husband, to have and to hold, to honor you, to treasure you, to be at your side in sorrow and in joy, in the good times, and in the bad, and to love and cherish you always. I promise you this from my heart, for all the days of my life.

The Exchange of Rings:

The wedding ring is the outward and visible sign of an inward and spiritual bond which unites two loyal hearts in endless love. It is a seal of the vows [Groom] and [Bride] have made to one another.

[Groom]: [Bride], I give you this ring as a symbol of our vows, and with all that I am, and all that I have, I honor you. With this ring, I thee wed.

[Bride]: [Groom], I give you this ring as a symbol of our vows, and with all that I am, and all that I have, I honor you. With this ring, I thee wed.

Declaration of Marriage: In as much as you have each pledged to the other your lifelong commitment, love and devotion, by the power vested in me by the state of _____, I now pronounce you husband and wife.

[Groom], you may kiss your bride!

Spiritual Wedding Ceremony

Although this is loosely based on Native American customs, it is a pure and holy service for anyone who wants loves the outdoors and wants a unique ceremony.

Dearly beloved, we are gathered here in the presence of nature, and before these friends and family, to join together this man and this woman in the honorable and beautiful estate of holy matrimony. Marriage is not to be entered into lightly, but instead with love, hone, friendship, and respect. These two persons present now come forward to be joined.

Intent:

[Groom], will you have this woman to be your wedded wife, to live together in holy matrimony? Will you love her, comfort her, honor and keep her in sickness and in health, in sorrow and in joy, and forsaking all others, be faithful to her as long as you both shall live?

[Groom]: I will.

[Bride], will you have this man to be your wedded husband, to live together in holy matrimony? Will you love him, comfort him, honor and keep him in sickness and in health, in sorrow and in joy, and forsaking all others, be faithful to him as long as you both shall live?

[Bride]: I do.

Celebrant reads the Cherokee Wedding Blessing during the Blanket Ceremony. You each are wrapped in a blue blanket, representing your pasts. After your union is blessed, remove your blue blankets so that your relatives can swaddle you in one white blanket to start your new life together.

Cherokee Wedding Blessing

God in heaven above please protect the ones we love. We honor all you created as we pledge our hearts and lives together. We honor Mother Earth and ask for our marriage to be abundant and grow stronger through the seasons. We honor fire and ask that our union be warm and glowing with love in our hearts. We honor wind and ask that we sail through life safe and calm as in our father's arms.

We honor water to clean and soothe our relationship -- that it may never thirst for love. With all the forces of the universe you created, we pray for harmony as we grow forever young together. Amen.

Vows:
[Groom]: [Bride], I love you today and I will love you forever. I will be faithful and kind to you for all the days of my life. This is my promise to you.

[Bride]: [Groom], I love you today and I will love you forever. I will be faithful and kind to you for all the days of my life. This is my promise to you.

Exchanging of Rings:
[Turquoise and silver jewelry are exchanged to protect against evils including poverty, hunger and bad luck.]
Love freely given has no beginning and no end. May these rings always remind you of the vows you have made.
[Groom]: I give you this ring as a symbol of my love. May it remind you always of this joyous day and these sacred vows. With this ring, I thee wed.
[Bride]: I give you this ring as a symbol of my love. May it remind you always of this joyous day and these sacred vows. With this ring, I thee wed.

Declaration of Marriage: Inasmuch as you have pledged yourselves to one another in love, compassion, and righteousness and confirmed your vows with the giving and receiving of rings, I am now honored to pronounce you husband and wife.
[Groom], you may kiss your bride.

Outdoor reception: Squash, beans, corn, fresh fruits in season, wedding cake are placed on a blanket, served buffet style.   None of the food is wasted. All of the food is either eaten or given away to parents, grandparents, aunts, uncles.

Catholic-esque Wedding Ceremony

These vows are for couples who for some reason are not able to be married in a Catholic church. A grandmother who traveled to Ohio from Philadelphia said that she understood that lay persons were contributing more and more in Catholic services. When I started to explain that I am a non-denominational minister, she stopped me and said she was happy that her grandson had a "real" church wedding.

Nuptials:

[Groom], do you come before us of your own free will to give yourself to [Bride] in holy matrimony? Will you love and honor her as your wife for the rest of your life? Will you lovingly accept any children as given to you as one of God's greatest gifts?

Groom: I will.

[Bride], do you come before us of your own free will to give yourself to [Groom] in holy matrimony? Will you love and honor him as your husband for the rest of your life? Will you lovingly accept any children as given to you as one of God's greatest gifts?

Bride: I will.

Catholic Wedding Prayer

Father, when you created mankind
you willed that man and wife should be one.
Bind [groom] and [bride] in the loving union of marriage;
and make their love fruitful so that they may be living witnesses to your divine love in the world.
We ask this through our Lord Jesus Christ, your Son,
who lives and reigns with you and the Holy Spirit,
one God, for ever and ever.
Amen.

Solemn Promise (Vows)

Please join your right hands as you declare your love and devotion before God and your guests.

Groom: I, [Groom] take you, [Bride] for my wife, to have and to hold, from this day forward, for better, for worse, for richer, for poorer, in sickness and in health, until death do us part.

Bride: I, [[Bride] take you, [Groom] for my wife, to have and to hold, from this day forward, for better, for worse, for richer, for poorer, in sickness and in health, until death do us part.

May the Lord in His goodness strengthen your consent and fill you both with His blessings. What God has joined together, let no man put asunder.

Prayer of Peace - St. Francis

Lord make me an instrument of your peace

Where there is hatred,

Let me sow love;

Where there is injury, pardon;

Where there is doubt, faith;

Where there is despair, hope;

Where there is darkness, light;

And where there is sadness, Joy.

O Divine Master grant that I may

Not so much seek to be consoled

As to console;

To be understood,

As to understand;

To be loved as to love.

For it is in giving that we receive,

It is in pardoning that we are pardoned.

And it is in dying that we are

Born to eternal life. Amen

The Blessing of the Rings:

The wedding ring is the outward and visible sign of an inward and spiritual bond which unites two loyal hearts in endless love. It is a seal of the vows [Groom] and [Bride] have made to one another. Bless, Oh God these rings, that [Groom] and [Bride], who give them, and who wear them, may ever abide in thy peace, living together in unity, love and happiness for the rest of their lives

The Exchange of Rings:

[Groom], [Bride], I give you this ring as a symbol of our vows, and with all that I am, and all that I have, I honor you. In the name of the Father, and of the Son, and of the Holy Spirit, with this ring, I thee wed.

[Bride]: [Groom], I give you this ring as a symbol of our vows, and with all that I am, and all that I have, I honor you. In the name of the Father, and of the Son, and of the Holy Spirit, with this ring, I thee wed.

Our Father who art in heaven,
Hallowed be thy name,
Thy kingdom come,
Thy will be done in earth, as it is in heaven.
Give us this day our daily bread.
And forgive us our debts,
as we forgive our debtors.

And lead us not into temptation,

but deliver us from evil:

For thine is the kingdom,

and the power, and the glory,

for ever. Amen.

Inasmuch as [Groom] and [Bride] have promised to each other their trust, fidelity and love in the sight of God and this company, by virtue of the authority vested in me as a minister of the gospel of Jesus Christ, I now pronounce them to be husband and wife, in the name of the Father and the Son and the Holy Spirit. Whom therefore God hath joined together let not man put asunder.

[Groom], you may kiss your bride!

Interfaith Marriage – Civil – Jewish

We are gathered here to celebrate the joining of this man, [Groom], and this woman, [Bride], in holy matrimony.

Marriage is not to be entered into lightly, but rather undertaken with great consideration and respect for both the other person and oneself.

Jewish Wedding Blessing

He who is the Al-mighty

and Omnipotent, over all;

He who is Blessed, over all;

He who is the Greatest of all;

He who is Distinguished of all;

Shall Bless the Chosson and Kallah.

Oh, God, supremely blessed, supreme in might and glory, guide and bless this groom and bride.

Intent:

Groom: Do you, [Groom], of your own free will and consent take [Bride] to be your lawfully wedded wife and do you promise to love, honor and cherish her throughout the rest of your life?"

Groom: I do.

Bride: Do you, [Bride], of your own free will and consent take [Groom] to be your lawfully wedded husband and do you promise to love, honor and cherish him throughout the rest of your life?"

Bride: I do.

Vows:

I, [Groom], take you, [Bride], for my lawful wife, to have and to hold, from this day forward, for better, for worse, for richer, for poorer, in sickness and health, until death do us part.

I, [Bride], take you, [Groom], for my lawful husband, to have and to hold, from this day forward, for better, for worse, for richer, for poorer, in sickness and health, until death do us part.

Exchange of Rings:

Groom: Behold, thou are consecrated unto me with this ring according to the law of Moses and of Israel.

Bride: Behold, thou are consecrated unto me with this ring according to the law of Moses and of Israel.

By the power vested in me by the state of _____ I now pronounce you husband and wife.

The groom crushes a glass with his right foot, and the guests shout "Mazel tov!" ("Good luck").

Love conquers all things; let us too surrender to love.

Virgil

———

CHAPTER TWENTY-FOUR

DIY Premarital Counseling

Whether you want conduct your own premarital counseling or would like to prepare for formal sessions, here is the general idea of the procedure.

Answer the questions honestly. There are no wrong answers. After you are finished, share the results and discuss anything that surprised you and areas where you disagreed. Do you see any patterns that you feel need to be addressed?

Family Background

- What are some of your favorite memories growing up?
- What family members were you closest to growing up?
- Were there any serious illnesses or deaths in your family when you were growing up? If so, how did your family handle them?

- How did your parents resolve differences of opinion between them?
- What values do you want to bring from your family into your marriage?

Finances

Unfortunately, finances are a large part of marriage and although far from romantic, they must be taken seriously.

- Are you both going to pursue careers?
- How could you handle a period of unemployment?
- How could you handle a poor credit score?
- Do you have stable employment histories?
- Do you have a savings account?
- Do you play the stock market?
- Do you keep your checking account balanced?
- Do you use credit cards? Do you pay them off every month or pay the minimum?
- List your outstanding debts including car payments, college loans, credit cards.
- List your current monthly expenses: rent/mortgage payment, utilities, insurance, credit cards, and all other loan payments.
- Do you donate to charity?
- Do you buy lottery tickets?
- If you won the lottery, what would you do with the money?
- Are you a spender or a saver?

- Do you have an emergency fund?
- Who will be in charge of family finances?

Emotion Intimacy

- What was the first thing that attracted you to each other?
- Are you able to talk about your feelings?
- Are there things that make it uncomfortable for you to communicate?
- Have you had any major disagreements? If so, how did you resolve them?
- Do you think you will stay married the rest of your lives?
- Are you comfortable with the way your partner expresses anger?
- Are you able to express your feelings with your parents?

Children

- Do you want children?
- How many children do you want?
- How far apart in age do you want them to be?
- How do you think children should be disciplined?
- Do you expect your children to get good grades?
- Do you expect them to be active in sports?
- Do you expect them to be popular?
- Will you raise them to believe in God?

- What if we can't get pregnant?
- Are there step-children coming into the marriage?
- What type of birth control should we use?
- How do you feel about adoption?
- How do you feel about abortion?

Family Life

- How will you spend week-ends?
- Would you ever go on vacation without your spouse?
- Do you want pets? Who will take them to the vet? Who will clean up after them?
- Where do you want to live? City? Suburbs? Country?
- Who will do the yardwork?
- How many nights a week should your family spend at home?
- Do you need time alone?
- What are your expectations about how we will spend our free time?
- Do you believe that we should be doing everything together?
- Can we each pursue our own interests?
- How would you feel if I want a night out with my friends now and then?
- How will we make sure we have quality time together?

Keeping Romance Alive

- What will you do to keep the romance alive?
- Will you continue to have date nights?
- How would a significant weight gain affect your relationship?

Two Hearts Beating As One

- Why are you getting married?
- How will your relationship change after you are married?
- How will it change if you have children?
- How will your relationship change if a relative has to move in with you?

Two Families into One

If you or your spouse have children:

- How would you describe a stepparent's role?
- What is the future stepparent's current relationship with the children?
- Is the other parent currently involved in the children lives?
- How will you make "dating time" for you as a couple without the children?
- What activities will you share with the children?

Housekeeping

- Will the groom "help" around the house or are you both equally responsible?
- How tolerant are you of messes?
- Is one of you substantially neater or messier than the other?

Health problems:

- Do either of you have health problems?
- How would you deal with serious health problems?

Criminal record:

- Have either of you ever been in trouble with the law?

Education level:

- Do either of you plan to continue your education?
- Are you happy with your level of education?

Family and holiday celebrations:

- Whose family will we visit at Christmas and other major holidays?
- How much time will we spend with our in-laws?

Faith:

- Do you think faith and spirituality are important in a marriage?

Your relationship:

- Do you think our differences will create problems in our marriage?
- Do you expect or want me to change?
- Are we both willing to work on our communication skills?
- Do we have problems in our relationship that we need to deal with before our wedding?
- Do we handle conflict well?
- How are we different?
- What can you forgive?
- What could you absolutely never forgive?
- Would you ever consider divorce as a solution to your problems?

Talk not of wasted affection; affection never was wasted.

Henry Wadsworth Longfellow

CHAPTER TWENTY-FIVE
Prison Weddings

Prison Weddings

As you know, an incarcerated person has few rights, and one thing he or she cannot demand is the right to marry. Some wardens allow weddings, and some do not.

One recently appointed administrator of a nearby facility believes it is in the best interest for an inmate to have a family waiting for his release. The chaplain prepares all paperwork and the bride goes to the court house to pick up the marriage license.

Before traveling to the prison for your wedding, make sure that you have followed all procedures. One bride called to cancel at the last minute due to a mix-up. The correctional institute has a "first visit" policy before there can be any marriage. Even though she and her groom had known each other most of their lives, due to the long distance to the prison from her home and her lack of transportation she had not visited him while he was incarcerated. During the eight hour trip, her friend's car was totaled when a deer ran out into the road. After all that, she was still not allowed to get married due to her not meeting the prison's strict rules. However, she is still determined to get married.

Since many prisons have rules regarding women's shoes, you may want to play it safe and wear loafers, tennis shoes, or low heeled pumps. Spike heels are not permitted in many prisons.

It is important to remember that modest dress is required. As a female guard explained to the bride and me, men are already "lonely" and too much skin will only exacerbate the problem. Revealing or inappropriate clothing is prohibited.

At one prison, I witnessed a woman wearing a sun-dress being turned away after driving four hours from Kentucky to Central Ohio.

No exceptions, no bare arms, no cleavage, no loaner clothing. Someone gave her four dollars along with a wish that she could find a clearance sale in a nearby store.

Also banned are shorts, hats, gloves, flip-flops and outfits that resemble prisoner or guard uniforms. If you are unsure if your clothing meets the requirements, call ahead.

Check the regulations before buying your rings. Some prisons allow plain bands only, no diamonds, not even for the bride.

When I first started visiting prisons I was shocked at how "cold" and "unfeeling" the employees (with the exception of one chaplain) were. Eventually I realized that they are following necessary protocol to keep everyone safe.

Prisons have strict regulations which must be followed. If weddings are allowed at all, they will be limited to specific days of the week and times.

One bride was discouraged from taking Wednesdays off as it is a vitally important day at work in her department, but Wednesday is the day reserved for weddings where her groom was incarcerated. She chose to put her personal Wedding of the Century ahead of her job without regret.

Brides are sometimes disappointed that their parents don't approve of the wedding. One bride called me at the last minute to cancel when her father refused to let her borrow his car.

One groom told me that he didn't deserve his bride and he had begged her to start a new life without him.

However, the joy of the event transcends the circumstances and the venue, and the weddings I've attended were cheerful.

One woman used a Bedazzler to spell out "Property of the Groom" on the back of her white t-shirt.

Another bride wore a long white gown topped by a white jean jacket. Her mother and sister accompanied her on the long drive to the prison and everyone celebrated with treats from the vending machine.

Here are a few things to keep in mind:

Don't bring unnecessary personal belongings. The prison I am most familiar with will not allow cell phones inside the main building. The prison additionally has rules against bringing money or gifts for inmates. Also, you may be searched at any time and any contraband will be seized. As long as you abide by the rules you have nothing to worry about.

No cameras are allowed which means there are no wedding photographs.

Remember to bring your identification.

Although physical contact is limited, inmates are permitted to hug and kiss their visitors. This means the groom is allowed to give his wife a brief embrace at the end of the ceremony.

Use your inside voice and be pleasant.

www.ingramcontent.com/pod-product-compliance
Lightning Source LLC
Chambersburg PA
CBHW070147290526
45789CB00002B/669